CRICKET PUNCH

MICHAEL BRUNER

REDHAWK
PUBLICATIONS

Cricket Punch

Copyright © 2024 Michael Bruner

All rights reserved. No part of this publication may be reproduced, distributed, or transmitted in any form or by any means, including photocopying, recording, or other electronic or mechanical methods, without the prior written permission of the publisher, except in the case of brief quotations embodied in critical reviews and certain other noncommercial uses permitted by copyright law. For permission requests, write to the publisher, addressed "Attention: Permissions Coordinator," at the address below.

ISBN: 978-1-959346-72-2 (Paperback)

Library of Congress Control Number: 2024946040

Any references to historical events, real people, or real places are used fictitiously. Names, characters, and places are products of the author's imagination.

Book design: Michael Bruner

Print Layout: Erin Mann

Printed in the United States of America.

First printing 2024.

Redhawk Publications
The Catawba Valley Community College Press
2550 Hwy 70 SE
Hickory NC 28602

https://redhawkpublications.com

MICHAEL BRUNER

a
Magic Enchantment
for
CHILDREN
trained
to produce
YET
Another
safe
Performance

7

CRICKET PUNCH

MICHAEL BRUNER

BELIEVE IT OR NOT

When you select THIS NEW Foreign Language

It's a way to clarify thought. and

make your *good* summer

GREAT

MICHAEL BRUNER

MICHAEL BRUNER

CRICKET PUNCH

So Branch Out you Travelling Companions OF the new generations

14

MICHAEL BRUNER

'GET HOLD OF

THESE

DAY-DREAM

EXPEDITIONS

MADE

TO

CHARMING SPOTS

and

LOST

horizons

15

CRICKET PUNCH

COUNT ON *it*

there are GUARDSMEN

on THE other end of the MOTORS

not allowed to ENTER THE LOOKING-GLASS

MICHAEL BRUNER

MICHAEL BRUNER

CRICKET PUNCH

20

MICHAEL BRUNER

THAT REFRESHES

and

says

"show us."

21

Forget the not quite bright enough Agencies THAT wash out THE SUPERLATIVE and ASSIST to STOP THE POSITIVE

MICHAEL BRUNER

CRICKET PUNCH

WITH Quality to carry over AND Comfort to Boot

IF only you dare to illustrate The Customs

CRICKET PUNCH

AS scenes made by MOTION PICTURE craftsmen For a feeling of confidence that gives What Stands Supreme its TOP TOUCH TUNING

MICHAEL BRUNER

and What Agents hide in The Chairman's finest speech

Announcing an event of great national importance and what it does to Our world

CRICKET PUNCH

CRICKET PUNCH

Do give direction **to** HOW **You** are FEELING **in** the mirror-surface

MICHAEL BRUNER

CRICKET PUNCH

CRICKET PUNCH

and **ONCE**

THERE

is

A

FOLK TALE

THE SUN NEVER SETS ON

THAT

helps

OUR CHALLENGED Heritage

YOU ORDER YOUR COPY

MICHAEL BRUNER

MICHAEL BRUNER

CRICKET PUNCH

MICHAEL BRUNER

CRICKET PUNCH

WHILE
the cheapest
regard
of the
Apparently white and
WHITER
Marketing Board
SYSTEM
speaks
IN
FRIGHTFUL
volumes
OF
CLEANER,
FRESHER,
SMOOTHER
every minute

MICHAEL BRUNER

CRICKET PUNCH

DO YOU   ARTIST

BRING that Certain Empire ?

CRICKET PUNCH

Are **You** THE NEW CHIVALRY of Stirring Deeds **&** Better ideas

OR THAT ever-present **LEGACY** of **WINTER'S** BEDLAM?

MICHAEL BRUNER

as The One in COMMAND DO you own

THE GREAT PRESCRIPTION THAT HELPS HEAL OUR future

or are you too CONFUSED by

the marks of winter

CRICKET PUNCH

MICHAEL BRUNER

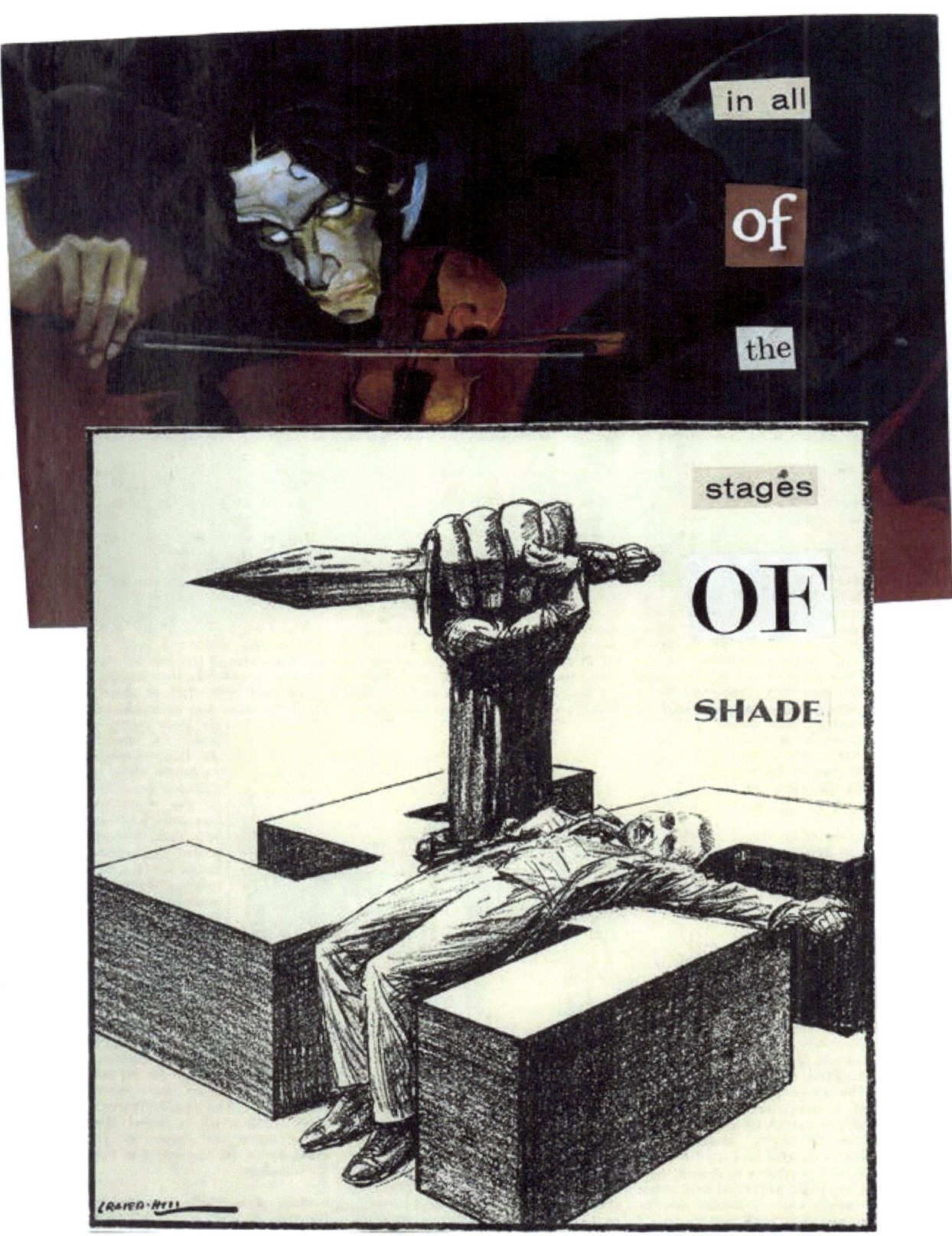

CRICKET PUNCH

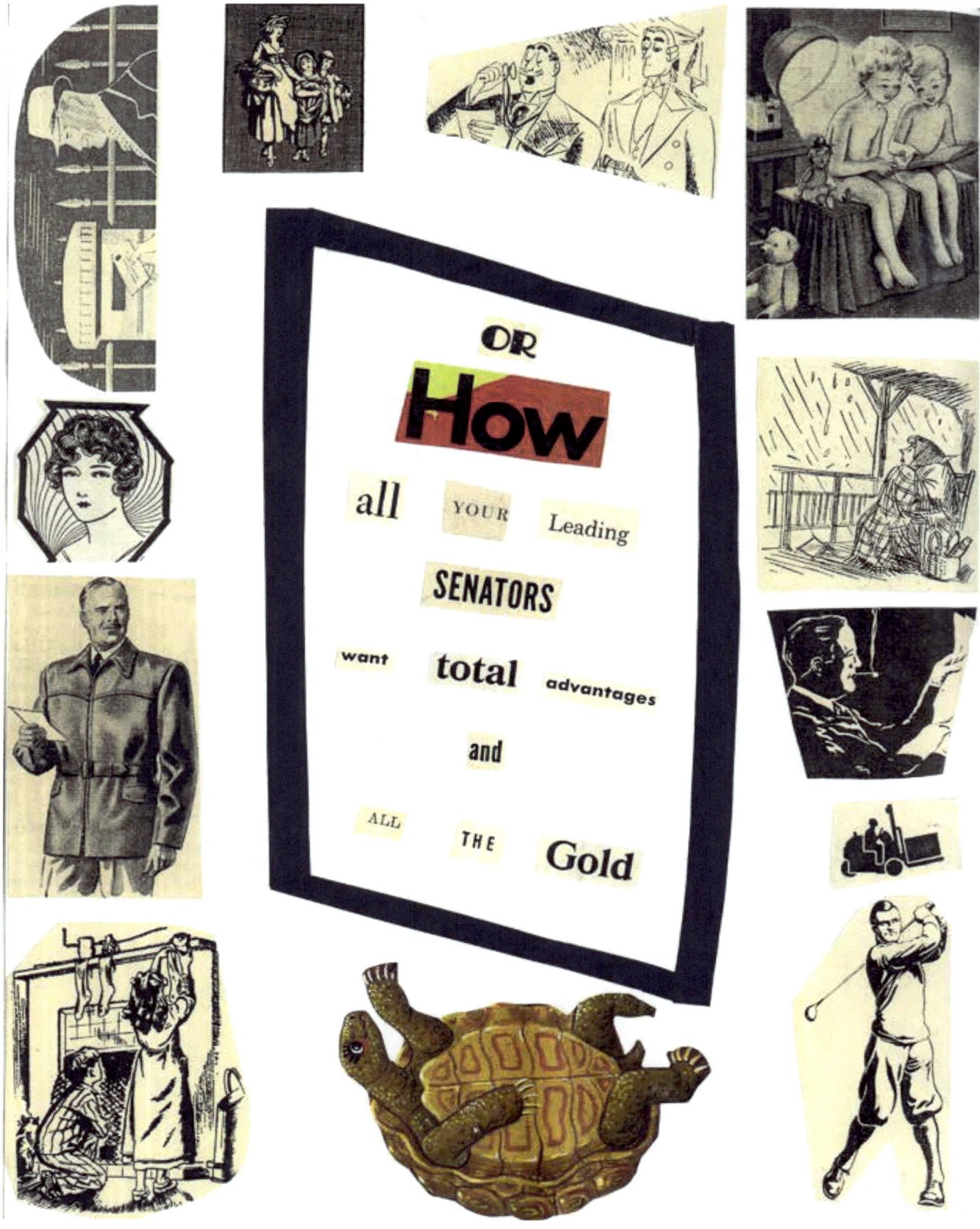

CRICKET PUNCH

MICHAEL BRUNER

AnD a way TO SAY What

even the eye cannot do

CRICKET PUNCH

56

MICHAEL BRUNER

CRICKET PUNCH

TRAVEL this WONDERFUL BRANCH OF Happy

MICHAEL BRUNER

SCIENCE *That* can't be observed in any other WAY

MICHAEL BRUNER

CRICKET PUNCH

FOR ANOTHER war is coming

and Here's one IN PROGRESS

and ONly A FEW can PREDICT THE PERVERTED JUSTICE

IN ALL THE great DEMOLITION WORK

CRICKET PUNCH

MICHAEL BRUNER

CRICKET PUNCH

MICHAEL BRUNER

CRICKET PUNCH

There's A TALE to be TOLD ABOUT Free between Making What's LOVABLE and

So DON'T get too

MICHAEL BRUNER

opinion **Ready to Branch Out** and *the* difference

The EFFECTIVE DISGUISE OF THE real ASSUMED BY the public

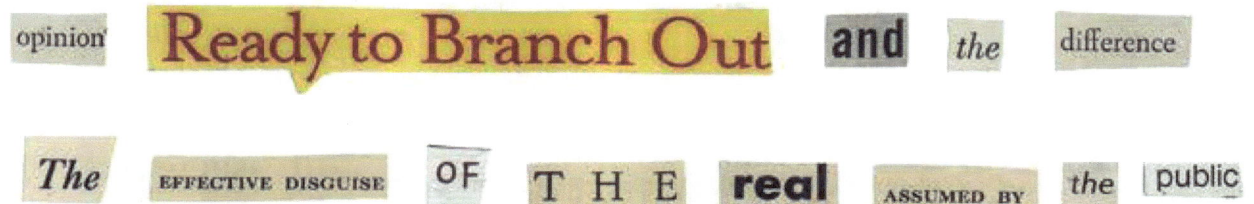

comfortable *with* the commonplace

CRICKET PUNCH

and be careful to look out for the subtle

charm of an Old Edition Taken for the new

CRICKET PUNCH

MICHAEL BRUNER

CRICKET PUNCH

74

MICHAEL BRUNER

CRICKET PUNCH

AND BE The HEALTH OF THE LIGHT

MICHAEL BRUNER

The Lost Tribe

(Sonnet found in a bottle floating in the Bermuda Triangle)

When to the sessions of sweet seersucker thought

I summon up remembrance of things lost,

Methinks of ye LOST TRIBE whose awesome Act I caught

Perchance in Piccadilly, or on the hot Venetian Coast;

For this TRIBE has wandered long in Space and Time,

Emitting brazen verse, and twinkling rhyme.

Whisp'ring in old Homer's ear, they moved his Hand,

And were the famous Haiku Bros. of old Japan.

Shall I compare them to a summer's day?

They are more lecherous and businesslike.

They spurred on the Charge of the Light Brigade

And told the Canterbury Tales to pay the mortgage.

    Through Space and Time they Warp along eternal,

    Four lads to Bard-dom born 'twixt God and Things Infernal.

A ditty by Douglas J. Kooth himself

MICHAEL BRUNER

For over forty years, *Cricket* magazine has delighted children, introducing them to the wonders of literature in an advertising-free manner, and Punch magazine, named after the anarchic puppet Mr. Punch of the old Punch and Judy shows, was a weekly magazine of humor and satire in London starting in 1841. In the spirit of the poetic power of dialectical images, it was an honor and pleasure to place pen and ink drawings from early *Punch* magazines in conversation with the lovely, more contemporary, graphics in *Cricket*. For, just as these two outlets introduced their readers to the wonderful power of language, this collage poem pursues precisely the same purpose via dialectical means.